Living Isaiah 30:18

Expect, Look, and Long for Him!

Dana E. Davin

PRESS

To Karen,

Thank you for the opportunity
to share the message! May we
live Isaiah 30:18 together!

In Christ,

Dara Davin

Acknowledgements

As a first-time writer, I truly believe that God wanted this message to get out. I thank the many who have given me their love and support as this book has emerged.

My love and heartfelt thanks goes out to my parents. I thank my Mother, Barbara Moorehead, who has loved me unconditionally all the days of my life and instilled in me the core values that guide my life today. Thank you, Mom for always being there for me, to listen or to talk, and for giving me pearls of wisdom just when I needed them the most. I also thank my father, Don Moorehead, who went to be with the Lord seven years ago. My Dad showed me the unconditional love and support of a father, and pointed me to the love that my Heavenly Father has for me. He was a Minister of the Gospel for over forty years, and the messages he taught me about a loving God who cares for me have changed my life! For both of my parents, I am eternally grateful!

Thanks to my Mother-in-Law, Dodie Peters, who is my angel on earth, who helps me with the practical everyday things, who helps me when I am down, who is always there when I need a listening ear or helping hand, and who always believes in me and encourages me. You are truly a gift from God!

Thanks to Lisa Richardson, my dear friend, who has always believed in me and who encouraged me to step out in faith and begin this journey of writing and public speaking! Lisa, God has used you to speak this new adventure of faith into my life. Thanks for seeing the vision before I did!

To my Pastor, Rod Loy, who has instilled in me that Every Soul Matters to God and that the Bible is our guidebook for living. All of the lessons you have taught me these past eight years, all of the teaching you have instilled in me, your incredible steps of faith as you "walk on the water" in so many areas of your life, made the writing of this book possible!

I thank Pat Knott, who read my rough drafts and gave me great feedback and encouragement! Pat is an author herself; the book that she wrote and published, *In Search of Kum Ba Ya*, gave me the faith to believe that I could publish my book! Thank you for paving the way, Pat, and for your great advice and encouragement!

To Joyce Meyer—you may not know me, but I am inspired daily by your teachings, your frank honestly, your amazing transparency, and your willingness to "talk turkey" to all of us about our part in this amazing journey of faith that we all travel together!

Thanks to all of my dear friends who read the book and supported me in my quest to share this exciting message of hope and love! Friends are a treasure in life and I truly treasure each one of you!

Preface

The writing of this book, *Living Isaiah 30:18*, is nothing short of miraculous! God totally wrote this book through me. That is why I cannot call it "my" book: this is God's book! Why did He choose me to write the book? I am not an author! The Word says that He deliberately chooses the foolish things of the world to confound the wise. So here I am, humbly offering this book to you!

This journey began a long time ago. I have been in direct sales for 25 years; my favorite part of the business is not the sales part, but rather the fact that I get to speak to and exhort women to be the very best they can be, to overcome their obstacles, both real and imagined, and to live life above their circumstances. I have known for over twenty years that my primary spiritual gift is the gift of exhortation; exhorting people, lifting them up, and encouraging them is truly my passion.

Having said all of that, here is the story.

In early January of 2010 I received news about a situation in my life that shook me to the core. Many of the beliefs that I had held near and dear were shattered, and I was rocked with mixed emotions. Part of me felt determined and full of faith, but another part of me knew that I had no control over the situation. I was left feeling confused and uncertain about the future. I went through periods of having great faith, but then great fear would come upon me. I found myself feeling paralyzed by that fear, and began to pray and ask God what He would have me do.

I kept hearing the words, "Be proactive!" in my spirit. I asked Him what that meant. All I heard was again, "Be proactive!" As we humans tend to do, I began trying to figure out what I was supposed to do. Nothing concrete came to mind but the words "Be proactive" played over and over again in my mind.

On January 25, 2010, I was crying and praying and feeling upset. I picked up my Bible and opened it to Isaiah 51 and 52. The words jumped off of the page: "Arise! Stand Up! Shake the dust off! Look to the Rock! Fear Not! Put on strength and might! Lift up your eyes to heaven! He will make my wilderness like Eden and my desert like the Garden of the Lord! The Lord will go before you and God will be your rear guard! My servant shall deal wisely and prosper! Humble yourself under the mighty hand of God and in due season you will reap a harvest, if you faint not!"

I heard Isaiah 30:18 for the first time on February 1. Oh, perhaps I had heard it before, but when I heard it that day, it was as if I was hearing it for the first time. Joyce Meyer, one of my favorite ministers on television, was teaching on this passage. The passage leapt off of the page and filled me with joy! I began to share the message with my co-workers, my friends, anyone who would listen! I was filled with faith and joy from the message of this scripture!

On February 3, I met with a friend to discuss the possibility of starting a ministry together. I went with my notebook and pen, expecting to discuss the non-profit venture we had been planning; in my spirit, however, I felt it was a great idea but not necessarily what *I* was supposed to do. However, I went ready to help with it in whatever way I could.

We got our food and sat at the table, when my friend looked me in the eye, took my hands in hers, and said, "We are not here to talk about what we had planned. We are here to talk about you!" She proceeded to tell me that she felt that it was time for me to step out in faith and begin being proactive about pursuing a public speaking ministry. I heard the word "proactive" and knew this was what God was referring to! I cried and felt butterflies, but I knew she was right. I had seen the vision of this many times before over the years, and I knew this was the path I was to pursue.

We talked about action steps I could take and arranged to meet again in one week to see what I had done. We would go from there.

I felt very excited, but wondered how this could come to pass. I kept hearing those words I had read in Isaiah 52, that said God would go before me and prepare a way, and that I was just to look to the Rock. So off I went! I contacted the people my friend thought I should, but got no response. That was fine. I knew this would happen according to God's timing, and I was at peace and still excited.

Friday night, February 3, I went to sleep as usual. In the middle of the night I woke up and the words, "Write a book" came to me. I thought "how crazy is that"? I tried to go back to sleep. Then I heard it again: "Write a book!" I lay there half asleep, still thinking how strange it was to be thinking such a thing, when suddenly words and sentences started pouring into my mind. I got my laptop, which was beside the bed, and began to type what I was hearing. That page is attached to this letter. Then I went back to sleep.

When I woke up Saturday morning I got my laptop and started writing the book, *Living Isaiah 30:18*. For four hours I did nothing but write; the words just came pouring out onto the pages. By the end of those four hours I had written about 8,000 words, and had the entire outline and basic "meat" of the book completed. Over the next twelve days, God would give me scriptures to add; I continued to tweak the book and write more. I believe the fact that God gave me this book in such a short period of time is due to the fact that this is a message that He urgently wants people to know.

Introduction

"And therefore the Lord (earnestly) waits (expecting, looking and longing) to be gracious to you; And therefore He lifts Himself up, that He may have mercy on you and show loving kindness to you. For the Lord is a God of justice! Blessed (happy, fortunate and to be envied) are those who (earnestly) wait for Him, who expect and look and long for Him (for His victory, His favor, His love, His peace, His joy and His matchless unbroken companionship)!"

—Isaiah 30:18

Uncertainty abounds in today's world. Everywhere you look, you hear of the struggling economy, out-of-control governments, the environment in peril, and wars raging. Even the strongest of Christians may struggle, feeling uncertain and disturbed about the future. But

God has not given us a spirit of fear; He has given us a spirit of love, peace, joy, and a sound mind (2 Timothy 1:7).

My prayer for you is that you be set free from the fear that may at times try to paralyze you and keep you in bondage, to the faith that gives ultimate freedom!

Isaiah 30:18 came to me at a time when I was struggling with fear, doubt and uncertainty. I had just received disturbing news about my future; fear, doubt and disbelief were attacking my spirit. God gave me this scripture, and it leapt off the page and flooded me with a new revelation that filled me with incredible joy and hope! I believe He gave me a revelation of each part of this scripture that will bolster your spirit and will help move you into the fabulous future that only God can give!

Imagine God earnestly waiting for you... expecting to be gracious to you...looking to be gracious to you...longing to be gracious to you and to me! Imagine God waiting, expecting, looking and longing to show you His loving-kindness! What in the world could be holding Him up? I believe He is waiting for us to earnestly expect, look and long for Him in our lives!

God has a message for you, a message of hope and encouragement that will lift you up and move you to an entirely new level in your relationship with Him and with others. He is earnestly waiting, expecting, looking and longing for us to expect, look and long for Him! Expect God to show up! Expect Him to fill you with His victory, His favor, His love, His peace, His joy and to give you His unbroken matchless companionship! That is the promise of Isaiah 30:18.

This passage of God's Word literally exploded inside of me! I pray that this message is a blessing to you and your life, no matter what you are going through!

In Him,
Dana E. Davin

Living Isaiah 30:18

Part I

Chapter One

God Waits

**"And therefore the Lord (earnestly)
waits (expecting, looking and longing)
to be gracious to you."**

In this first part of Isaiah 30:18, God is waiting—but what is He waiting for? This verse says that He longs to be gracious to us, but He is still waiting. I believe He is waiting for us! He is waiting for us to expect, to look, and to long for His grace and mercy! He is waiting for us to look, long for, and expect His loving-kindness! He is waiting for us to look to Him! You see, this relationship with the Almighty Creator of the universe is a two-way street!

Many times we tend to treat God like a magic genie living in a bottle that we keep on a shelf until we have a need. Then we pull the bottle off the shelf, rub the bottle, and expect God to pop out and grant our requests. But God longs to have a real relationship with us, an intimate daily walk with Him. Relationships only work if there is give and take; two people (or in this case one person and our God) in unity, "relating" with one another.

God is waiting for us to look up...to look to Him...to expect Him to answer when we cry out to Him! That should be a simple thing to do, but so many times we instead spend our days looking at and dwelling on our circumstances. We fret and worry and wonder and ask God why. We often make ourselves sick with worry; we become fatigued and discouraged because the answer doesn't come quickly. That's what fear, doubt and disbelief do to the human spirit that lives within us! When our spirits are in tune with God's spirit, we can take on those feelings of doubt and uncertainty that try to overtake us; we can walk with a confidence that isn't based on circumstance! Our confidence has to be in God and His ability to work through us even when we don't feel adequate or qualified! I like to call that "God confidence"—when we don't have the "self confidence" we need, then we call on the God confidence that is readily available to us when we call out to Him and expect Him to show up.

When I find myself worrying and focusing on my problems rather than the promises of God, I remind myself that God isn't in Heaven wringing his hands with a furrowed brow, saying, "Oh, what am I going to do about this situation? I had *no idea* that this was going to happen!" In fact, that picture of God is so funny that it makes me smile just thinking about it. Imagine God worrying over your situation! Try to imagine Him pacing back and forth, rubbing His brow and fretting! Ridiculous picture of God, isn't it? Then think about it the next time worry tries to overtake you. If God isn't worried about your situation, and He already knows the answer to your problem, then why are you worrying? Circumstances are subject to change; why not believe that they will change for the better? He is earnestly waiting, expecting, looking, and longing for you to call on Him for your answer and God is not worried!

The Disciple Matthew had a lot to say on the subject of worry!

Matthew 6:27 says: "And who of you by worrying and being anxious can add one unit of measure (cubit) to his stature or to the span of his life."

Matthew 6:31 says: "Therefore do not worry and be anxious, saying, what are we going to have to eat? Or, what are we going to have to drink? Or, what are we going to have to wear?"

The key word in this passage is "saying". When we are worried or anxious we often say things that are negative or self-defeating, but we need to remember that the words we speak hold power!

Proverbs 18:21 says: "Death and life are in the power of the tongue, and they who indulge in it shall eat the fruit of it [for death or life]."

The words that we speak hold power over us, so when we feel anxious or worried, a key element for us as overcomers is to watch what we say. Instead of speaking the worry, doubt or fear you may feel about yourself and your situation, instead learn key scriptures and speak those verses about your life and your situation! Just speaking the uplifting message of the Gospel will lift your spirits. When you are feeling more optimistic, you are more likely to make better choices regarding the things you can control. When it comes to the things you can't control, well…that's where faith comes in. We either trust Him or we don't!

Hebrews 11:1 says, "Faith is the substance of things hoped for, the evidence of things unseen."

If we can see the answer, then it doesn't require much faith, does it? When we can't see what lies ahead, and the future seems uncertain, that's when faith certainly comes in handy! Build up your faith by filling your mind with the promises of scripture. When we focus on what

God says about our situation instead of what people say or what we see with our own eyes, faith will rise up in us and give us a renewed peace and strength that we might not have had otherwise.

Once again, Matthew is talking about worry when he says in Matthew 6:34: "So do not worry or be anxious about tomorrow, for tomorrow will have worries and anxieties of its own. Sufficient for each day is its own trouble."

When we spend our todays worrying about what may happen tomorrow, we often miss the blessings that are waiting for us that day. Often, the very things we are worrying about never come to pass anyway!

I remember when my son, Michael, was little. When we had an appointment to go to the doctor he would ask me over and over, "Mom, am I going to get a shot?" I would tell him that I didn't know if he would or not, but if he did get a shot, the pain would be very short-lived. He would often ask me again, "Mom, do you think I'll get a shot this time?" I would watch him worry over that possibility until he made himself sick. Many times he never got the shot anyway; when he did, the pain was very brief, as promised. Think of how many days he suffered, worrying about those sixty seconds of possible pain that many times never came at all.

I think about that from time to time when I find myself worrying about something in the future that "might" happen. I have to remind myself of what I told Michael years ago: that very thing we worry about may never even come to pass! Why miss out on being peaceful and happy today, instead worrying about the "shot" that may or may not happen in the future? Why not think on the possibilities of great things to come for your future?

You may be thinking at this point, "Well, that sounds really great, but I can't help it! I come from a family of worrying people! I am just a worrier by nature!"

The Word says that you can help yourself! It actually says in 2 Corinthians 10:5, "We demolish arguments and every pretension that sets itself up against the knowledge of God, and we take *captive* every *thought* to make it obedient to Christ."

This passage says we can take our thoughts captive, which means that we do ultimately get to choose what we think about! I remind myself of that scripture when I find myself worrying and focusing on the problem rather than on the promises of God. We can't keep those worrisome thoughts from entering our minds, but we can keep them from building a home there!

Instead of worrying about things we can't control, things that may or may not happen, let's focus on what God promises us in Isaiah 30:18: God is waiting to be gracious to us! Grace is God's favor imparted to us, and the God of grace and mercy is waiting to answer our prayers! But He is waiting for us to do our part: for us to expect, look, and long for Him to show up, to earnestly expect Him to move on our behalf!

I often hear people say about their situation, "Well, I guess all we can do now is pray!" But why would we make prayer the last resort? Wouldn't that be the first thing we would do? But all too often, instead of turning it over to God, we try to fix things on our own, independently and without help. Then we try enlisting the assistance of others to help with the situation. It is only when all of our best efforts have failed that we turn to God for help! God is asking us to make Him our first resort, to make prayer the *first* thing we do, to be dependent upon Him right away instead of using our independence to get ourselves in a deeper mess before we cry out to Him.

I have learned that God is a true gentleman. He will never force Himself on us. He gives us a totally free will. We get to make the choice of how we want to live our lives; He will never try and make us do what He wants. God's love never fails. He longs for us to look to Him as our source. He tries to get our attention over and over again. We get to choose to listen or to ignore His voice because God will never force us to serve Him. He waits for us to make the decision. He has already chosen us. The question is, have we chosen Him?

And so He waits—patiently, lovingly, earnestly—for us to come to Him, with our joys and our sorrows, with our requests and our heart's desires, with all of our flaws and faults and imperfections. His grace is sufficient. He already knows what we need before we ask. He already knows the answer, and isn't surprised by who we are! He already knows everything about us, what we will do and what we will need. He created us, after all, and He asks us to come to Him just like we are...as my Mamma always said, "Warts and all!"

Chapter 2

God Lifts

"...And Therefore He lifts Himself up, that he may have Mercy on You and show loving-kindness to you..."

Imagine God lifting Himself up! I was trying to picture that in my mind, and the vision that I received was that of God stretching Himself upward and looking down toward us! I can't imagine God laying down or even sitting! Can you? But if God says that He lifts Himself up, then the point is that He is moving, lifting, shifting—and it's all because of us! The verse says that He lifts Himself up so that He may have mercy on you and show loving-kindness to you! Wow! You are that important to him! He longs to have mercy on you and on me! Mercy isn't given to us because we did something to deserve it; mercy isn't conditional. Mercy is God's unmerited favor, freely given to us. God's mercy is unconditional.

The ultimate example of God having mercy on us and lifting himself up is when Jesus was lifted up onto the cross at Calvary, stretching His arms out in love to embrace us and to forgive all of our sins. While hanging on that cross He forgave those who put Him there. He forgave the thieves who hung on either side of Him, and He forgives each of us now! That is showing loving-kindness and mercy in its truest form! This gift was given freely, and now He earnestly waits for us to receive that gift as a true revelation in our spirits and in our hearts!

As human beings, it is difficult to imagine showing mercy to someone who doesn't deserve it. People hurt us and disappoint us, and we tend to hold on to that hurt and disappointment. We wait for an apology, for them to "deserve" our mercy and loving-kindness. But God calls us to show mercy and loving-kindness before the apology, even if it never comes at all. If our goal as Christ-followers is to be like Him, then we don't have a choice in whether or not we have mercy on others.

We absolutely want God's mercy in our lives and we long for Him to show us His loving-kindness, don't we? The God-given challenge is to step up and out and begin to show that same mercy and loving-kindness to others! God is waiting for us to be different than the world, because we are the only picture of God the world may ever see! My question to you right now is this: If you were the only representative God had on this earth, would the people put in your path want to know more about Him? Would they look at your life and your behavior and say, "Man, I have to get to know this God that she (or he) serves!" That is truly our ultimate goal in life as followers of Jesus Christ…to be "Christ-like" and to point people to Him!

Now you may say, "But I could never be like Christ! How is that possible?" God's Word says that the same spirit that lives in Jesus also lives in us; we can do all things through Christ who strengthens us. Therefore, being like Christ has to be possible! The key to showing mercy and loving-kindness to those who haven't done any-thing to deserve it is to do so "through Christ". In and of yourself, you can't do it. It isn't possible to live that kind of life without Christ living in and through you. It all goes back to expecting Him to show up. Ask Him to live in and through you so you can do things that in your own human capabilities would never happen!

2 Corinthians 9:8 says: "And God is able to make all grace abound to you, so that in all things at all times, having all that you need, you will abound in every good work."

The Word says in *all* things, at *all* times we will have *all* that we *need* and will abound in every good work. It doesn't say we will have everything that we *want* in everything that we do, but it does say we will have all that we *need* for every *good work*!

Wow! That Word from God fills me with the confidence that I need to do the good works He has given me to do! Let it bolster you up with the confidence that you need to do the good works He has set before you! It is His grace that is sufficient when our strength is gone! It is His grace that abounds when we don't think we have the talent or ability to pull off something that we feel led to do! Lean on God's grace and expect God to lift Himself up on your behalf! He is earnestly waiting and looking for you to turn away from the circumstances....to turn away from your inability and to His ability, to look away from the hurt and pain that other people may have caused, to look away from the mountain in your life that seems so insurmountable! He is earnestly waiting for you to look up and expect Him to be gracious to you so that you can impart that same grace to others! Doesn't that sound like true freedom?

No one ever said it would be easy. That is why we must "live and move and have our being" in Him (Acts 17:28). God lifts Himself up that He may have mercy on you and show loving-kindness to you; in the same way, we lift ourselves up and become more Christ-like in our behavior towards our fellow man.

How long will we let ourselves be kept down by bitterness and choosing not to forgive others? Keeping score is exhausting. Being angry on the inside while trying to fake forgiveness on the outside will cause fatigue (and you may even find yourself struggling with depression). To truly be set free, we must lift ourselves up and show mercy and loving-kindness to others! Feel the freedom that comes from that lifting up and from that mercy! Isn't that truly what you want?

Choosing not to forgive is simply choosing not to show mercy to others. But if we fully embrace living the life of a Christian, a Christ-follower, then not showing mercy to those who don't deserve it or who haven't earned it isn't a choice we can make. If mercy is God's unmerited favor and forgiveness shown to us, and we want that mercy in our lives, then we have to show that same mercy to others. Therefore, we can't wait until someone deserves our forgiveness to show them mercy.

Not forgiving others when they have hurt or disappointed us also keeps us in bondage. The offending party goes on living life and may not even be aware that they have hurt us, or they may be aware but not care. Regardless of what they choose to do, we must choose the path of forgiveness if we are to be truly free in this life. Not forgiving others keeps us in bondage. Not forgiving others for a long period of time can cause a root of bitterness to take hold in our lives. That lack of forgiveness can hold us back from being all we were meant to be! I encourage you now to release that person or event that hurt you. Let go of the anger, bitterness or resentment that have held you captive for far too long. Forgive and be set free! Forgive as Christ forgave you, even when you did nothing to deserve it! Forgiving someone isn't about them—it is all about us! It isn't a gift you give to them—it is a gift you give to yourself!

Colossians 3:13 says: "Bear with each other and forgive whatever grievances you may have against one another. Forgive as the Lord forgave you."

Mark 11:25 says: "And when you stand praying, if you hold anything against anyone, forgive him, so that your Father in heaven may forgive you your sins."

That sounds like pretty serious stuff! He is telling us to forgive others so we may be forgiven! And if He is telling us to do it, then it must be possible to forgive. You may not feel like forgiving, but we are in big trouble if we live our lives based on our feelings. Forgive whether you feel like it or not. You choose to forgive as an act of your will, not your emotions. You forgive because you want others to forgive you when you mess up. You forgive because you want God's forgiveness. Forgiveness isn't a feeling. Forgiveness is a choice.

We know that we reap what we sow! In the same way that God lifts Himself up to show *us* mercy, so we must lift ourselves up and show mercy and loving-kindness to others. That is a lifting that will change your life and the lives of those around you! Who do you need to forgive? Who needs your undeserved mercy and loving-kindness? You will truly be set free to live life on an amazing new level once you lift yourself up and choose the path of mercy!

God lifts Himself up on our behalf. He is lifting Himself up even now, and He has his eyes on you! He is ready to see you live the life you were truly called to live! He is expecting you to do great things! He is looking and longing to show you His grace, His mercy, His unmerited favor; all He is asking is for you to do the same for others.

One day when I was having a pity party (have you noticed no one ever wants to come to those parties?), God gave me the scripture Isaiah 60:1: "Arise (from the depression and prostration in which circumstances have kept you...rise to a new life)! Shine (be radiant with the glory of the Lord), for your light has come and the glory of the Lord has risen upon you!" Then I read Deuteronomy 31:8: "I am the Lord your God and

I go before you and I will be with you. I will never leave you or forsake you. Do not be afraid! Do not be dismayed!"

Basically He was saying, "Get Up! Shake the dust off! Fear not! Move forward! Put on My strength and might! Rise above your circumstances! I am going before you and I will be with you! Don't be afraid!" I knew it was a message for me on that day and at that moment. God spoke to my heart and told me that if I am to run the race He has set before me, I have to GET UP! He told me to lift my eyes toward Heaven and start expecting Him to do something great on my behalf! He also told me that He would go before me and make a way for me! What an awesome Word from God! He is speaking that very Word to you today!

We want everything to turn around quickly once we rise up and move forward, but we have to sit up before we can crawl, crawl before we can walk, and walk before we can run! Start now by looking up, rising up, and moving forward, and you'll be running the race that God has set before you in no time, with faith and power and knowing that God has already gone before you to prepare the way! Don't wait for things to be perfect! I encourage you to start today! Arise, shake the dust off, move forward and be lifted up to a new level of power in your life! It will be the power of God living inside of you!

Chapter 3

God is Just

"For the Lord is a God of justice."

This part of Isaiah 30:18 says that the Lord is a God of Justice. He is fair and gives us due rewards. He longs to bless us and move on our behalf when we are faced with injustice in our lives, but He cannot continue to bless us while we live in disobedience. It just isn't in His nature, because He loves us too much to let us continue going down the wrong path and not attempt to stop us or derail us from this path.

Have you ever tried and tried to do something in your own strength, and no matter what you did, how great you were, how committed you were, nothing seemed to work out right? Have you ever prayed and prayed for God to intervene and do something on your behalf, but saw nothing happening and wondered why? I believe that God withholds blessings in certain situations that He knows are not right for us, when He knows we are heading down a path that will lead to our ultimate demise or something that is less than His best for us. He may let us go and not intervene for a time, but He loves us too much to just leave us alone and let us continue moving in the wrong direction! Perhaps the obstacles you are facing are because of your own disobedience, or this could just be an indicator that it is time for God to take you in a new direction. Pray and ask God what He is doing. He will give you the answer in His perfect timing.

In these times of testing and trials, these times of discomfort, perhaps God is unfeathering your nest. What, you may say? Unfeathering my nest? Yes! In life, there are seasons for some endeavors, but then those seasons come to an end. Perhaps you have been greatly blessed in some area of your life, but suddenly you seem to hit one roadblock after another. When those challenging times come, they may be simply a test of your faith and determination. Perhaps persistence or a different approach will work. Obviously, success doesn't happen overnight in many situations; sometimes we can experience great success for a season, then have a time of testing, and then have great success in that area again. But sometimes I believe God is moving us out of our comfort zone and into a new direction.

God often speaks to me using nature and His creation. This time of discomfort reminds me of what happens in a young bird's life. When a bird is a baby, the mother bird creates a nest that is soft and full of downy feathers. The baby bird feels safe and warm in the nest. The mother bird brings the food and feeds the baby, and it is well provided for. But when the mother bird senses that it is time for the baby bird to test its wings and fly from the nest she prepares it to leave by slowly removing the downy feathers one by one. She stops bringing in the abundant food that the baby bird has come to depend upon. Suddenly the nest isn't so soft and warm. The bird begins to feel the twigs underneath him, and he becomes uncomfortable. The bird feels hunger pains and he begins to look out over the side of the nest to see what is beyond the world that he has known since birth. This uncomfortable situation is the catalyst that motivates the bird to shake out his wings and give them a try. This is the only reason the bird decides to embark on the new adventure—the new life that the bird was meant to have!

Imagine if that mother bird never removed the downy feathers from the nest. Imagine if she continued to feed the bird big fat worms, and kept the baby bird in that nest. The bird's development would be thwarted and its plan and purpose would never unfold. Eventually the bird would die in the nest. I believe God sometimes acts as that mother bird does, causing our lives to change in ways that make us try new things and head in a new direction.

Sometimes it is very painful when God moves us in a new direction. As human beings, we don't love change. We tend to enjoy what is familiar and what feels safe. We want to stay in our nest where we feel a sense of comfort and security. Unfortunately for us, growth equals change; it calls for us to get out of that comfort zone—to get out of the nest and fly!

Galatians 6:9 says, "In due season we shall reap a harvest, if we faint not!" The key is to not faint during the process of reaping the harvest... during the process of leaving the nest...during the test!

God has a history of repaying our trouble with multiplied blessings. Isaiah 61:7 says, "Instead of your (former) shame you will have a two-fold recompense. Instead of dishonor and reproach (your people) shall rejoice in their portion. Therefore in their land they shall receive double (what they had forfeited); everlasting joy shall be theirs."

My interpretation of this verse of scripture is that, when we have experienced great loss, God will restore what the enemy has taken from us.

God is just. He knows what has happened in your life that may have been unfair or uncalled for. This means that we don't have to spend our days trying to vindicate ourselves; God is our vindicator!

Perhaps you did nothing to cause the problem you are facing. God is just, and He will repay and restore. We don't know when or how; we just know that He will. His timing is perfect—God doesn't operate in our time frame! Maybe the problems you are facing are because of poor choices that you have made. God is still a God of justice. When we acknowledge the part we played in the mess we are in, and we repent and turn to begin walking down the right path, God sees that. He knows your heart. He is a God of justice! He will set things right. That doesn't mean we won't suffer consequences from the choices we make, but He is always working on our behalf. When we are walking with Him, He will cause what was meant to harm or destroy us to work for our good in some way.

Genesis 50:20 says: "You intended to harm me, but God intended it for good to accomplish what is now being done, the saving of many lives."

This verse lets us know that what happens to us in life, the struggles we go through, the problems and the tough situations that we face, can be used at some point in the future to help someone else! If we never went through trials, how could we ever identify with a hurting world? How could we relate to others, and help lift them up and encourage them when they are going through their trials? Everything that happens to us in life is meant for our ultimate good. When we go through trials and come out on the other side, we can help others make it through too!

The goal is to remember that God truly is just and He is a God of double blessings—a double portion! We may not see this happen quickly, but when we expect, look and long for Him and continue to do what He has called us to do, I believe blessings do come to us! Justice is God's hand of fairness and right dealing, working in our lives. When we follow His direction, His justice will follow. He knows exactly what you need. He knows how to take you there. As we wave the white flag of surrender to Him and give Him full reign over our lives, we can trust Him to gently lead and guide us in the right direction in life. We can then be a shining light to help someone else along the way! One life blesses another as we experience God's justice in our lives!

It is important for us to be thankful as we wait for God's justice. Thanking God and praising Him even in the midst of a time of trial or injustice is critical.

1 Thessalonians 5:18 says, "Give thanks in all things and in all circumstances, for this is God's will for you in Christ Jesus."

Ephesians 5:20 says, "Thanks be to God who always causes us to triumph."

So we give thanks to God, knowing that He has our ultimate good in mind. We thank God when everything around us is falling apart. We thank God when we pray and don't get an immediate answer. We thank God when we are walking down a path we didn't expect and didn't want to travel.

Have you ever had something terrible happen, and at that moment felt overwhelmed, dismayed and afraid? Later in life, have you been able to look back and see how something good came from that awful event? Often, events happen in our lives that seem insurmountable at the time, but in retrospect we can see that the event, which was so difficult to go through, actually gave us a gift that we wouldn't have otherwise received.

When I was in my early 20's I lived in an apartment that caught fire in the middle of the night. My son and I escaped with our lives, but nearly everything of material value that I had in that apartment was lost. I remember feeling numb and wondering how I would recover from that terrible event. I later looked back and realized that had I not lost the goods I had in the apartment, I would never have moved to a new location; that move ultimately took me to a place where I surrendered my life to God, and found the business that I have loved for over 25 years. Looking back,

I can now see how that fire took me down a path that I would not have taken otherwise.

Sometimes we go through trials that we never understand. It is in those circumstances that we trust God and thank Him for who He is. We thank Him for being with us when things go terribly wrong. We thank Him for holding us up with His mighty hand when we would have fallen down without Him. The Word says to be thankful in *all* circumstances. When we know that God is a God of justice, we can trust Him even when we can't see the good that can come from what has happened to us or those we love.

I don't believe God causes the tragedies in our lives, but I do believe that He can take those tough situations of life and ultimately bring us out on the other side. He is a God of justice, and He can make right what went so terribly wrong—or He can just hold us in the process.

Because the Lord is a God of justice, we too observe justice in our dealings with others.

Psalm 106:3 says: "Blessed (happy, fortunate and to be envied) are those who observe justice (treating others fairly) and who do right and are in right standing with God at all times."

I don't know about you, but I want to be blessed, happy and fortunate. Don't we all envy those who are? When we treat others fairly and do the right things, regardless of the situation and how we are treated, then we receive the blessings, the happiness, the great fortune that comes to us when we live life on God's terms instead of our own!

Thank God for His justice in your life. Because He is in us and we are in Him, we are the just and we can be in right standing with Him. Hebrews 10:38 says: "But the just shall live by faith." Knowing that God is just and that we are just because of Him gives us the ability to go through every situation with faith and trust, abandoning the fear that once kept us in bondage. "He who the Son sets free is free indeed!" (John 8:36).

Thank God for the justice in our lives!

Chapter 4

We Wait

"Blessed (happy, fortunate, to be envied) are all those who earnestly wait for Him..."

Waiting just isn't fun! We want what we want and we want it NOW! The beginning of Isaiah 30:18 states that "God waits (expecting, looking and longing)". Well, if God can wait, then I suppose we can too! This verse also states that we are blessed, happy, fortunate, and to be envied when we earnestly wait for Him! So we know that we will do some waiting! The key to waiting is to wait "well". How do we do that? Isaiah 40:31 says, "They that wait upon the Lord (who long for, expect for and hope in Him) shall renew their strength!" So we know that we wait upon the Lord, and according to this passage the waiting brings about good things—but while we wait we are not passive! We wait with longing, expectancy and hope! We are excited while we wait because we know that God is moving on our behalf, even when we can't see it or feel it!

I remember a season when my business was struggling and I was compelled to begin working more and longer hours than ever before. I was tempted to give up aspects of ministry that were important to me, but God spoke to me and said, "You take care of my business and I will take care of yours!" I didn't see an immediate turnaround in my business, but I continued to do what God called me to do as I waited for Him to show up on my behalf. He has never let me down!

The Word says that the trying of our faith worketh patience. No one likes the trying times of life, but they truly are where our faith is built. Anyone can praise God when all is going well, but when we are in the waiting process and nothing seems to be happening...well, that is truly when we find out what we believe. It is where our true nature and character are revealed. We have to learn to wait with patience and to wait "well". Patience is about how you act while you are waiting. The truth is, we will all wait at some point in life, but how well will we do our waiting? Can we wait with joyful expectation? Yes, we can: when our hope is in God and not in people or circumstances. That is the key to waiting well.

Sometimes in life, bad things happen, one after another. When you have had a series of tough things happen to you and have been going through a prolonged period of waiting while living in negative circumstances, you can find yourself still waiting for the other shoe to drop. Instead of anticipating blessings, we start wondering what else will go wrong. We say things like, "If it weren't for bad luck I'd have no luck at all" or "the only appointments I seem to have are disappointments!" or we talk about Murphy's Law: "Anything that can go wrong will go wrong!" During these times of multiple difficulties, tests, and trials, we certainly acknowledge that life is tough; however, it's more important to speak about God's promises during tough situations.

Instead of giving the negative situations a voice, build up your faith while waiting on God by quoting His Word over your situation: "And my God shall supply all my needs according to His riches in Glory by Christ Jesus!"(Phil. 4:19) "I can do all things through Christ who strengthens me!" (Phil 4:13); "Greater is He who is in me than he who is in the world!" (1 John 4:4); "By His stripes I am healed!" (1 Peter 2:24)

Find the uplifting promises of God in your Bible that truly speak to your heart regarding your situation, commit them to memory, and begin saying them out loud. Your faith and confidence in God will begin to build! Your mind doesn't always differentiate between truth and a lie, so watch what you say. Your mind will begin to believe what it hears repeatedly!

I have two little Pomeranians who are like my children. One is rather passive and submissive, and the other, Katie, has the most amazing determination I have ever witnessed. When Katie wants something from me, she is relentless! The look on her face is one of joyful expectation when she first begins to "ask" for what she wants. If I don't respond quickly enough, she sits on her hind legs, puts her paws in the air, and begs in a most charming manner. If I am still slow to respond to her urgent plea she looks at me with a very serious expression, and then the barking begins. She rarely gives up until she gets my attention and moves me into acting on her behalf.

When I watch Katie's persistent and determined attitude, I am reminded of Mathew 7:7: "Keep on asking and it will be given to you; keep on seeking and you will find; keep on knocking and the door will be opened to you".

I often wonder what would happen if we were that determined to get God's attention. What if we truly desired for God to move on our behalf, or on behalf of someone we are praying for so strongly that we never gave up? We often pray a few times but quit when we don't see a manifestation of God moving how we want Him to, thinking He isn't listening or doesn't want to answer us. Why is it that we give up so easily, taking the path of least resistance and often walking away without continuing to pursue the answer to our prayers? Many times when Katie is begging, asking, and pleading for me to respond I have every intention of doing so, just not in her time frame! I believe that is often true of God Himself. He has every intention of answering our prayers and petitions, just not always in our time frame. There is usually a lesson to learn in the waiting, but as we wait we continue to expect, look and long for God to answer our prayers!

I recently heard one of my favorite ministers say that the enemy is in charge of all of the "dis-" words: disappointment, discouragement, despair, and disillusionment. The bottom line is that we all get disappointed at times, but we have the choice to release the disappointment, realizing that there are going to be things in life that hurt us. We can choose to move past them. Discouragement, despair and disillusionment can set in when we hold on to disappointment. The Bible says that we have a choice in these matters. We can "take every thought captive" and see these negative thoughts for what they are, or we can keep them, nurture them and let them build a home in our heads! The Bible also says that "we have the mind of Christ" so we can choose to think His thoughts and replace the negative thoughts with the pure, the powerful and the priceless thoughts of God! The only way to accomplish this task is to meditate on the Word of God which has the power to transform our thinking!

When we take our eyes off ourselves and wait upon the Lord, we become stronger! The fatigue begins to lift and we feel hopeful, because our hope isn't in our situation or circumstances, in people or in things! Our hope is in Him, who is able to lift us up and move us into unspeakable joy, regardless of our circumstances. Even though the circumstances may not change, we can still have joy, peace, and feel that victory is coming when we look and expect the Lord to show up!

You may be feeling like you are the main problem, and perhaps you are, but I recently heard someone say that "whatever is wrong with me isn't big enough to stop God!" He is able to use my weaknesses to confound the strongest of men! If we were able to do it all through our own strength and ability, then how could He bring forth His power in and through us? It is in our inabilities that He is able to perform the greatest miracles! Rejoice in your weaknesses because He will show up and do more than we could ever think to ask! You do what you are able to do, and He will do the rest. Take your natural and add His super, and see the supernatural happen in your life! He isn't looking for perfection; He is looking for our willingness to follow Him in every area of our lives!

I encourage you today to come to the end of yourself. Take your eyes off your circumstances; wait with a spirit of expectancy. Be relentless in your pursuit of God! Expect Him to respond to you! Look for His amazing provision. Long for Him to fill you with His love, faith, and hope for the future! He is earnestly waiting for you right now, right where you are, to look up and begin expecting Him to move and act! He will give you everything you need while you are going through difficulties, while you are waiting!

While waiting, find ways to focus on joy! It is human nature to want to "wallow" in our problems, to talk about our circumstances to everyone who will listen, but I encourage you to acknowledge the situation without giving it too much power over you. While going through tough times, you won't feel like being joyful. You won't feel like praising God, but Nehemiah 8:9 says that "The joy of the Lord is your strength"! We need joy and strength for the journey while we wait! Listen to music that lifts you up, watch and listen to messages that fill your mind with the amazing truths of God's Word. Listen to inspirational stories about other believers who have walked a similar path and have come out on the other side! Joy will begin to rise like a flood inside of you! You and I must actively build up our faith by taking these steps. Choose to rejoice as an act of your will, and your mind and emotions will follow the path of joy. The joy you are choosing will bolster your spirit; your strength will rise, and you will be waiting well!

Chapter Five

We Expect

"Expect, Look and Long for Him..."

In this part of the verse God is calling us to expect, look, and long for Him! Expecting is another choice we get to make, but what are we expecting? Are we expecting great things to happen for us and our loved ones? I believe our expectations are often based on what has been happening in our lives lately. Are we expecting another disappointment, or perhaps more bad news? When life gets tough and we are faced with the choice of what to expect, we must remind ourselves of the big picture. When challenging times come our way, we tend to look at is the negative things that are right in front of us—but whatever we focus on expands! It seems like the more you focus on the negative aspects of life, the more negative comes! Take a moment to look at your life and see it in a broader sense. Many times, just looking at things from a new perspective gives us a chance to see things in a new light!

I love the example of a woman who is "expecting" a baby. At first she cannot see or feel the baby growing inside of her, and she isn't even aware that she is expecting—but she is. The baby grows inside of her for months. She is expecting, but she still can't see the object of her expectations. She may experience morning sickness, fatigue, and heartburn—unpleasant side effects of the amazing miracle that is to come—but she's still joyful because she's expecting that baby and is willing to pay the price! It would be silly to deny that she is expecting a baby, even though no one has seen that baby! We know it is there! We anticipate its arrival! We prepare and plan and even name the baby! But we haven't seen the baby with our own eyes!

Your future is just like that. You are "pregnant" with something amazing that God wants to do in you and through you, but you can't see it yet. At first you don't even feel it, but then something happens and you begin to feel a stirring inside of you that God is up to something. The process of "birthing" what God is doing may be unpleasant at times. There may be side effects to the waiting period while you are expecting your breakthrough, but they don't mean God isn't working to bring it to pass. Go through life expecting what is to come with great anticipation! Be willing to pay the price for your amazing future! Be willing to see and possibly feel nothing at times during the waiting, but know in your spirit that it is coming!

While you wait, be of good courage—be brave! Psalm 27:14 says, "Wait and hope for and *expect* the Lord; be brave and of good courage and let your heart be stout and enduring. Yes, wait for and hope for and *expect* the Lord!" If we really trust God and know that He has a plan for our lives, then why wouldn't we be of good courage? But the key word here is "enduring". Anyone can wait well for a short period of time. We often pat ourselves on the back for waiting so well for something that took a few weeks or maybe even a few short months. But what happens when it takes years and we don't see anything change? Can we endure such a wait; can we be of good courage and continue to expect God to move on our behalf? Psalm 31:24 says, "Be strong and let your heart take courage, all you who wait for and hope for and expect the Lord!"

Once again, we are being told to be strong and take courage. This verse says we will have to wait—but we continue to wait with expectancy!

Remember that our hope must be in God and not in people—not in a job or career, not in our bank accounts, but in God Almighty! How cool is that? He cares so much for us that He says to wait and expect and that we can have our confidence in Him! Psalm 39:7 says, "And now, Lord, what do I wait for and *expect*? My hope and *expectation* are in You!"

Two of my favorite words in the Bible are *"But God..."*! I notice that over and over again when the children of God are in trouble, when their backs are against the wall and all odds are against them, the Word says, "But God..."— and here comes their deliverance! I really try to live a "But God" kind of life. When trials come and times are tough, when nothing seems to be working and I can't see a way out, I have begun to say to myself, "But God..."! Ok, God...I am expecting you to show up to work this situation for the good! Study the "But God..." moments in the Bible and be encouraged. He specializes in doing the seemingly impossible, or at the very least the improbable! Then, when the situation turns, people turn to Him and can see Him at work in their lives!

Expecting God to show up is just part of this faith journey we are on. Sometimes we feel full of faith and power, and other times we feel weak and our faith dwindles! When faith seems far away, when God seems far away, remind yourself of all the times that He came through for you. Look back at the victories that you have won in your life. Think of the times when you didn't think He would come through for you, but He did anyway. Remember that faith is believing in what you can't readily see with your own eyes. If we could see the answer we wouldn't need faith. Part of being God's child is trusting that He has our best interest at heart, even when the answer to our prayers doesn't manifest itself right away. Trust that God is teaching you something valuable in the process. Expect His goodness to manifest in your life! Trust His heart even when you can't see His hand!

Expect God to speak to your heart and give you His wisdom and direction! Expect God to move on your behalf in His perfect timing! Expect God—that's it: EXPECT GOD! He is earnestly waiting for you to expect Him to show up! In fact, He's already there!

Part II

The Result of Living
Isaiah 30:18

We now know that God earnestly waits, expects, looks, and longs to be gracious to us! We now know that He lifts Himself up so that He may have mercy on us and show us His loving-kindness. We know that God is a God of justice! We know that He expects us to do some things too: He expects us to earnestly wait, expect, look and long for Him; He expects us to show mercy and be gracious to others. The result of our doing these things is nothing less than spectacular! Let's break down the awesome benefits of earnestly expecting God to show up, of waiting well and of looking and longing for Him! Let's look at the rewards that God promises when we live Isaiah 30:18!

His Victory

We receive His Victory! According to the Merriam-Webster Dictionary, the word "victory" means, "the overcoming of an enemy or antagonist; the achievement of mastery or success in a struggle or endeavor against odds and difficulties." Princeton's online dictionary defines victory as "the successful ending of a struggle or contest". God says He will give you victory: the successful ending of your struggle!

We know that our ultimate victory was obtained by Christ when He went to the cross to die for us! We know that the ultimate victory will be seeing Him face-to-face, but while we are living on this earth, we can still expect to have victory!

That doesn't mean that there will be no trouble. The Bible says that the rain falls on the just and unjust alike (Matthew 5:45), but it also says that "Greater is He Who is in us than He who is in the world!" (1 John 4:4). This teaches us that we can live victorious lives even in the midst of the struggle or trial we may be facing. Victory in our lives doesn't require that everything goes our way. True victory comes when we live overcoming, faith-filled lives, even when we face those challenges that inevitably come because we are human and live in this world!

When I ask people how they are doing, they will often answer, "Well, under the circumstances..." and then proceed to tell me of their trouble. I often wonder what they are doing "under" their circumstances to begin with! As Christians we are called to live above, we are called to go higher, we are more than conquerors through Him who loves us (Romans 8:35-37)!

When we are "problem-focused," the situation can seem insurmountable to us! What we choose to focus on expands in our lives; when we focus on the problems we are facing, they can become all-consuming. It is so easy to stay problem-focused unless we meditate on our answer. Choose to fill your mind with messages of hope and victory! Listen to CDs, read books, and watch programs that will uplift and encourage you. "As a man (or woman) thinketh in his (or her) heart, so is he (she)!" (Proverbs 23:7). We—no one else—are in charge of our thinking, and we renew our minds daily by focusing on the answers and the solutions rather than ruminating on the problems!

God says He has given us His Victory. If He has given this victory to us as a gift, then let's receive that victory and walk in it today! Choose right now to become a *victor,* not a *victim,* as you journey through life! You will not only see your own life change, but you will be a light that shines so others may follow and find victory in their lives as well!

His Favor

We receive His Favor! Favor is "unmerited blessing"! How exciting! We don't have to deserve His favor—He gives it to us when we expect, look and long for Him! The Bible refers to the favor of the Lord over and over again, especially in Genesis and Exodus. In most cases, favor and blessings go hand in hand, and favor is divinely given. Look for and expect divine favor to follow you in your dealings with people and situations.

Ask God for divine appointments in every area of your life, and watch for them to come your way!

Exodus 33:17 says, "And the Lord said to Moses, I will do this thing also that you have asked, for you have found favor, loving-kindness and mercy in my sight and I know you personally and by name."

No longer do we have to walk this earth trying to do things in our own strength, using just our talent and personality alone! He goes before us and walks with us!

Some people are more "gifted" with people or "talented" in business than we are. Wouldn't it be a shame if they were the only ones who could garner favor? Because God is imparting His favor to you, it doesn't matter if you are the most "talented" person on the planet. When He is imparting His divine favor to you, then you can accomplish great things even when "talent" may be lacking!

We often think that when we have done something wrong, we lose God's favor. That isn't true—God knows your heart! Repent and He is faithful to forgive!

Psalm 30:5 says, "For his anger lasts only a moment, but His favor lasts a lifetime; weeping may remain for a night but rejoicing comes in the morning!"

He longs to forgive us! When we have repented and have forgiven others for what has been done to us or our loved ones, we can rest assured of that forgiveness. He is looking to give us His divine favor!

Walk in loving-kindness, be merciful to others, and ask God with confidence to give you divine favor, with every person and in every situation! He longs to impart that to you, for He knows you personally and by name! Expect it! Look for it! Long for it!

His Love

We receive His Love! The unconditional love that never fails becomes a daily part of our lives, and when we have His unfailing and unconditional love we can impart that loves to others!

How difficult it is for us to truly walk in unconditional love. As humans, we put conditions on people. We determine if they are deserving of our love, and then sometimes we give love to others based on our feelings. But love is a choice, and God has chosen to give us His love so we too love others as an act of our will.

1 Peter 4:8 says, "Above all things have intense and unfailing love for one another, for love covers a multitude of sins (forgives and disregards the offenses of others)".

But God also wants us to love Him with our whole hearts! Deuteronomy 6:5 says, "And you shall love the Lord your God with all your (mind and) heart and with your entire being and with all your might."

Love is a choice! So as we choose to love God with all of our hearts, we love others with an unconditional love that can only come from God's Holy Spirit dwelling inside of us!

The world today would have us think that love is a feeling, but true love is the choice to love in spite of feelings. Feelings fluctuate. The feelings of love can come and go. If we wait until we feel like loving someone, we may have a long wait—we could miss out on amazing blessings! Real love is shown when we love in spite of the way we are treated! Real love is evidenced when we choose love regardless of the other person's behavior or response to us. God's love, which can truly become a part of who we are, is the kind of love that calls us to love no matter what. That doesn't mean you have to like someone in that moment, or like what they have done in a particular situation. But liking and loving are two entirely different things. Love is not a feeling. Love is a decision you make. Love is a choice!

(Remember that loving someone doesn't mean you have to take abuse from that person. You can love someone and still choose to remove yourself from a situation. You can love someone as a person, but not love their behavior. You can choose not to allow them to continue to be abusive to you or someone you love.)

This love that God imparts to us is supernatural! The more we lean on Him and His power and divine abilities that are at work within us, the more we renew our minds through the Word of God, and the more we let those Words of faith and power build up inside us, the more we are able to walk in perfect love. Perfect love casts out fear, so the more love we have, the more we can take on the image of Christ! As we expect, look, and long for God in our daily lives, we receive His love in full measure!

There is a Christian folk song from the '70s that says, "They will know we are Christians by our love, by our love, yes they'll know we are Christians by our love!" That God kind of love will transform us and will show the world around us that we truly belong to Him!

His Peace

We receive His peace! God's peace is the peace that surpasses human understanding. It's a supernatural peace that comes in spite of circumstances. It is truly a peace that cannot be easily explained to others. It just is!

John 16:33 says, "In Me you may have (perfect) peace and confidence. In the world you will have tribulation and trials and distress and frustration; but be of good cheer (take courage; be confident, certain, undaunted); for I have overcome the world!"

When we have His peace we can have confidence! We can take courage and be certain and undaunted!

I have always said that self-confidence comes and goes and can be affected by circumstances, but God-confidence is steady and stable and consistent! When we don't have confidence in ourselves, we can be confident in God and still have His peace!

The NIV translation of the Bible translates Isaiah 26:3 as, "You will keep in perfect peace him whose mind is steadfast, because he trusts in You." That same scripture in the Amplified Bible reads: "You will guard him and keep him in perfect and constant peace whose mind (both its inclination and its character) is stayed on you, because He commits Himself to You, leans on You and hopes confidently in You."

So the big key to having peace in life is to keep our minds fixed on God and on His Word.

John 14:27 says, "Peace I leave with you; my peace I give you. I do not give to you as the world gives. Do not let your hearts be troubled and do not be afraid."

God says that He give us *His* peace! He tells us not to *let* our hearts be troubled. That means we have a choice!

Colossians 3:15 says, "Let the peace of Christ rule in your hearts, since as members of one body you were called to peace. And be thankful."

Isn't it interesting that this passage links the peace of Christ to our being thankful? It's difficult not to have peace when we have a thankful heart!

As you commit your life to Him, lean on Him! Hope in Him and look to Him, expecting Him to pour out His grace, mercy and loving-kindness to you. He will guard you and keep you in perfect and constant peace! I am expecting that today; how about you?

His Joy

We receive His joy—joy that is unspeakable and full of glory! The joy that cannot be explained! The joy that floods our souls in the very darkest of nights and the very best of days!

Sometimes we confuse joy with happiness. I truly believe you can have unhappiness in your life and still be joyful. I believe that you can go through tough times and trying circumstances and still choose joy! Joy is that inward knowledge that no matter what may happen, you can never be shaken from the hand of God! Joy is the outward manifestation of what is living inside of your heart! Joy, like love, is a choice and shouldn't be based on our situation or circumstances. Besides, joy gives us strength!

Nehemiah 8:10 says, "Do not grieve for the joy of the Lord is your strength!" When you find yourself in a battle, put on praise music, dance and sing! Choose to do the exact opposite of what you may feel like doing, and watch your strength rise! The joy of the Lord is your strength; when you lose your joy you lose your strength!

Psalm 5:11 says, "But let all those who take refuge and put their trust in You rejoice; let them ever sing and shout for joy, because you make a covering over them and defend them; let those also who love Your name be joyful in You and be in high spirits."

No one is denying that there will be times of pain, hurt, fear and uncertainty. We all struggle with the feelings that try at times to overtake us, but God is saying DON'T STAY IN THAT PAIN! The Word says to take refuge and put your trust in Him! He isn't saying to deny that the pain exists or that you feel the way you do; rather, He is saying to focus on Him instead of focusing on the pain! He is saying to expect Him, look for Him, long for Him, and you can receive His joy that transcends the pain of your current situation!

Psalm 16:11 says, "You will show me the path of life; in your presence is fullness of joy, at Your right hand there are pleasures forevermore."

As we remain in His presence, we have fullness of joy! Receive that joy today!

His Matchless, Unbroken Companionship

When we live out Isaiah 30:18 in our daily lives, we find ourselves living in true unbroken companionship with God Himself. When we earnestly expect Him, look for Him, and long for Him, then He comes to dwell inside of us—we are transformed. Our lives become attractive to others as they see the love and light of Jesus shine through us. In Joshua 1:5, He promises us that He will never leave us nor forsake us. What a promise!

What an amazing, personal, loving, merciful God we serve! How can we not look to Him with joyful expectancy, with a longing in our hearts to truly see Him as He is: so glorious, so loving, so merciful and forgiving? How can we not want to serve this amazing God?

I am reminded of the song we often sing at Easter: "He lives! He lives! Christ Jesus lives today! He walks with me and talks with me along life's narrow way! He lives! He lives! Salvation to impart! You ask me how I know He lives. He lives within my heart!"

God is walking with you. He is talking to you. He longs to be your constant companion. Sense His presence right now. He knows you. He is there with you. He loves you. He forgives you.

Hebrews 13:5 says, "Never will I leave you. Never will I forsake you."

Deuteronomy 31:6 says, "Be strong and courageous. Be not afraid or terrified, for the Lord your God goes with you; He will never leave you nor forsake you."

How amazing that the God who created the universe promises never to leave us! He is offering us His matchless unbroken companionship! He wants to be *your* companion! He wants to converse with *you* and walk with *you* and hold *you* in His arms!

He created us to be His companions and to do His work on earth. When we long for His presence and come to realize that apart from Him we truly can do nothing, then we can enjoy our lives on this earth without worry or fear, and with His *matchless unbroken companionship* as a part of our daily lives.

In Summary

Isaiah 30:18 is truly a life-changing verse of scripture! As we live out this scripture, God comes to live in us and dwells in us fully—we are never the same! When you understand that God is earnestly waiting for you, that He is looking and longing to be gracious to you and to show you His loving-kindness, that He longs to show you mercy and provide justice in your life...when you get that picture in your mind, then God is no longer some mythological creature who lives on high and is unreachable and unfathomable! He becomes your friend, your champion, your companion, your Savior! When you realize just how much He thinks of you, how much He loves you, how much He longs for you to come to Him, then you will find yourself falling in love with this God, this Jesus, this one who never fails!

As we earnestly wait for Him, look for Him and long for Him—as we learn to wait well and behave properly in the process, as we walk through the world with His victory, His divine favor, His love, His peace, and His joy no matter what our circumstances—then we will live a life that is truly worth living. People will be attracted to and fascinated by us; we will be able to point them to the source of this amazing life we have found: the Holy One, Jesus Christ and His amazing life-changing power!

God has given us everything we need to accomplish this goal! He has given us His attributes! The choice now is to receive what He has given us, and live a life that is truly worthy of the name Christian. A dying world is waiting for us to step up, lead by example, and show them the way! Live Isaiah 30:18 and live it well! God is earnestly waiting for you!